ROTTEN POETRY FISH

ROTTEN POETRY FISH

by

Hume Cronyn

Mosaic Press
OAKVILLE, ON - NIAGARA FALLS, N.Y.

Canadian Cataloguing in Publication Data

Cronyn,Hume, 1957-
  Rotten Poetry Fish

ISBN 0-88962-711-8

1. Title.
PS8555.R6112R67 2000   C811'.54   C99-932855-7
PR9199.3.C6683R67 2000

Published by MOSAIC PRESS, P.O. Box 1032, Oakville, Ontario, L56 5E9, Canada. Offices and warehouse at 1252 Speers Road, Units #1&2, Oakville, Ontario, L6L 5N9, Canada and Mosaic Press, 4500 Witmer Industrial Estates, PMB 145, Niagara Falls, NY 14305-1386

Mosaic Press acknowledges the assistance of the Canada Council, Ontario Arts Council and the Department of Canadian Heritage for their support of our publishing programme.
ISBN 0-88962-711-8
Printed in Canada

Le Conseil des Arts | The Canada Council
du Canada | for the Arts

MOSAIC PRESS, in Canada:
1252 Speers Road, Units #1&2,
Oakville, Ontario
L6L 5N9
Phone / Fax: 905-825-2130
cp507@freenet.toronto.on.ca

MOSAIC PRESS, in USA:
4500 Witmer Industrial Estates
PMB 145, Niagara Falls, NY
14305-1386
Phone / Fax:1-800-387-8992
cp507@freenet.toronto.on.ca

ACKNOWLEDGMENT

Some of the poems in this collection have appeared in the following publications: *Dog, Foolscap, Iron, Rustic Rub, Slow Dancer.*

CONTENTS

I

II

III

IV

I

CHRISTMAS BLUES

When the snow lies in patches on my easy chair,
when my room grows stuffy like a herd of deer,
when Christmas hangs down my back like a wet tongue,
I flee from my room, I walk through parking lots,
inhale the sweet perfume of aluminium carbide,
trudge under bridges kicking at frozen puddles,
snap off the jovial moods growing from my shoulders,
scatter them like weeds,
I wail till the stray cats line up in procession behind me,
and when I come across Santa I beat him with a pack of chewing gum,
leave him an ironing board to dissect the dishonesty of his ways,
wrap him in nudity to protect him from the snakes,
warn him about the gold leaf that rots the tree,
refrigerate the sob that explodes from his hot burly body,
he understands like a splinter from a broken mirror,
thanks me for my birdhouse contributions,
while tears freeze on his cheeks like fences,
I call my cats, they come down from the birches,
with salty tongues, they lick the fences from his face,
I point out that the manger and the three wisemen have failed,
what comes down the chimney goes up in smoke,
sometimes white hair equals snow,
but I'll look for Christmas elsewhere.

Rolled

If a man breaks you in two
and wants three pieces.

If a man pries open your throat
and pours down a crown of thorns.

If a man pulls the children from your eyes
and stuffs your sockets with a barren sky.

If a man drags a train through your belly
and talks about the redemption of walking.

If a man plants a bed of fatigue in your forehead
and salts the wind with one, and only one, truth.

If a man pulls a tree from your lungs
and crumples a few dead leaves in your pocket.

If a man wraps your love in a white-hot fist
and hocks it at the first pawnshop of the lamb.

If a man marches a procession of words over your tenderness
and proclaims that it is the army of healing.

If a man regales you with the laws of the holy city
and wrings the flowers like a dirty sponge.

If a man takes your sea and fills it with sand
and breaks the mast of your sailboat.

You know he's talking about God and eternal salvation,
the seven deadly sins and the testament of revenge.

You know he's talking about eternal forgiveness,
eternal damnation, the all-embracing love of God.

Omniscient! Omnipotent! Omnipresent! Beyond dispute!
Beyond comprehension! Beyond common sense! Beyond life!

You know that when you burst out screaming,
when you carry your head under your arm,

when you tear out your heart with nail clippers,
you know you've been rolled by one of God's messengers.

TERMITES

This is what I have to say:

The termites bit into the church as if it was birthday cake and the steeple
      fell like a candle.

It's nobody's business what the termites were doing (unless you happened
      to be the unlucky person crushed by the falling steeple.)

I want to say one thing about the windows:

It was a small country church and children, stuffed at the end of pews,
had noses pressed hard against the glass, the sermon pounding into its
      twenty-fifth minute.

What did they see?

They saw that the grass was impeccably cut. Saw that the trunks of the
      chopped-down trees had been freshly tarred.
Saw a crow that was squawking as if it had swallowed a toy soldier.

The sermon droned on about Christ's pain on the cross,
and that regardless of the words He uttered He never felt abandoned.

The children longed to see a blade of grass that had not been decapitated.
They longed to see a tree bursting out in a spangle of green.

They longed to build a tree house from the boards they had collected.
They longed to sprinkle the floor with grass (if grass had to be cut, they'd
      make use of it).

The sermon was wrenched to a conclusion that if Christ suffered so much,
      what did our pain amount to?
And that each time we suffered — no matter how unjust — resurrection was
      granted through it.

The children dreamed of securing a rope from the branch above the tree house,
and swinging (of course, the tree overlooked a river) through the air

and with an exhilarating whoop, letting go of the rope,
and splashing kerpppppplunk!!!! into the river.

The minister had taken out his handkerchief, was coughing copiously.
It was the end of the sermon. Two hymns to go.

KERRACCCCKKKKK!!!!

Who would have ever guessed that the collective effort of generations of
        termites would strike at this moment?

PEARS

Please don't disturb!
A man in here
Is eating some lettuce
And a fruit
With the most delicate ears.

Pears
Hear everything that is said.
They must be eaten in silence.

With a knife
Cut stairs
That wind around the pear.
Walk up the stairs
With a candle:
The flicker of light
Is lost in the white pulp.
Nothing is seen.
Nothing is heard.
All is taste.

Taste
That sweeps through the body,
Grows larger than the body,
Encloses
The body in one large pear.

Shhh!
That man is a pear.
Few people know such a delight.

AROUND THE POOL

Airplanes fly back and forth tugging a string of letters with advertisements
such as CONFETTI RED HOT REGGAE PARTY TONITE. LADIES
DRINKS FREE. You can only read the letters in one direction.

A man gets out of the pool in a bathing suit that looks like a lime-green
diaper, goes over to his girlfriend, shakes his wet hair all over her, she
goes inside and gets his lime-green sunglasses.

A little girl in the pool holds up a sailboat with red sails, 'Mummy, can I get
out?' Mummy, sprawled on a deck chair, the Miami Herald covering her
like a beach towel, is sound asleep.

I'm sitting on the patio of our hotel room, a low hedge separates me from the
bathers around the pool, the waves of the ocean are drowned out by
the rinse cycle of the dishwasher, my mother-in-law is talking to a
lizard.

The wind tears at the flags of five countries, but the tops of the royal palms
are barely moving.

Every few minutes a bather sits up and vigorously slathers on more sun tan
lotion.

Some very fat bodies have stepped into bikinis and are wisely lying down.

Even men in their twenties have paunches.

The ceaseless drone of airplanes.

A sand crab scoots under my chair heading for the open door, but when he
takes his first step onto the carpet, my mother-in-law whacks him with
a newspaper.

The pregnant woman appears earlier than usual, I have never seen a woman
look so sad in pregnancy, but today she takes off her sand-coloured
pullover, revealing a bathing suit of the subtlest marine-blue with a
flamboyant red bow.

A helicopter flies overhead, two children run as if they were going to hit the
deck, a little boy drops his pail.

My wife and daughter stand at the gate, they have returned from the beach,
they dip rags in turpentine and scrub off oil that wodges up between
toes, cakes heels, streaks legs, spots hands.

The sand crab has moved next door, a little girl pokes it with a stick, her
mother says, 'Don't, you must be kind to the fish and crustaceans.
They were here before we were.'

A lizard darts under the hedge, plates clatter as my mother-in-law starts to
unload the dishwasher, I bury my head in a biography of a Russian poet.

GIDDY-UP

Grandma sits in her easy chair.
In a blue chiffon dress,
immaculately lipsticked,
she reads her romance.

Her two grandsons ride
the back of her couch.
'Giddy-up,' they shout, 'GIDDY-UP.'

Grandma reads her romance.
She is waiting for her dead husband's
brother to pick her up for dinner.

Her grandaughter, on the other side of the room,
has pulled on her ice skates, is tying up
the laces.

Grandma reads her romance.

Her daughter kneels in front of the fireplace,
hypnotically watches the kindling burst into flames.
She has just had an argument with her husband.

Grandma sips from her tea,
then sinks back into her romance.

One of her grandsons is about to fall off the couch,
her grandaughter to stand up and walk across the rug in her skates,
her daughter to plunge her hand into the fire.

Grandma, three pages from the end of her romance.

The boy falls off the couch,
smashes his head against the window.
The little girl skates across the rug.
The woman moves closer to the fire.

Grandma puts down her romance,
'In Patagonia they found true love.
They eloped, riding horses across the pampas.'

Her daughter stuffs a newspaper into the fire.
Tomorrow they'll take the kids to the zoo.

Red and Green

The dishes are piled.
The children are in the living room.
We talk in the falling light.

Talk about.

Chloe and her first week of school.
How tired we are. The cost of a monthly pass.
Who's going to phone the repairman?
What are we going to do for Phil's fortieth?

The screech of trains fills the room.
A lighbulb shines brightly, then goes out.
The tap is dripping. The picture on the wall
is losing its detail in the growing dark.

With nothing on but a diaper,
Blake appears at the end of the hall,
runs towards us,
whooping with delight,
ee-ai ee-ai ee-ai

when he reaches the kitchen,
he turns, runs back down the hall,
two pairs of mittens are
caught around his foot
— mittens on strings —

they bounce up and down
red and green
bounce up and down
ee-ai ee-ai ee-ai

red and green

green and red

commas to an ongoing sentence,
while you and I, slumped in chairs,
are caught in full stops.

STRANDED

Between the wall with leaves dropping like hearts and the desk that smells like a tired old root, I have followed the nightman. If it was not for his hats, worn out as the moon, and the leg that he left behind in the oozing mud — now hard as cement — I would have lost him years ago.

Not that you'd be proud of me. Most of the time I spend sitting in white chairs. Sometimes you'll find me hiding under them. I hate myself when I start eating the carpet.

My quest is for the floorboards. It's such a waste to ignore the wonderful gift of bare feet. We were born to have the rough taste of wood rub up against our toes. Of course, I don't underestimate the chance of slivers.

And it doesn't help that my fingernails are pared so close to the quick.

If you were perceptive, and sometimes even I miss it when I look in the mirror, you'll see that I have a collection of small droplets beneath my eyes.

No matter how small you are, they are not deep enough to dive into.

So fuck you, nightman! I feel as if I'll always be stranded in this desert. So what if you've left me your leg, like a signpost in the dry and cracked mud.

What good is it? I need two legs to walk to the lake with mirror-like stones.

SHADOW MAN

In the evening when the grass lies down like a rotting pair of pyjamas

the man with the shaved head and the vagrant look arises from his bed with 2000 years of make-up and a crown with several names

he has bells on his shoes and a history of bad mistakes, and his pockets — which have no room for his hands — one of them bulges with a change purse full of bottle tops

he has no pretensions, he wanders midst the sirens and the skid row streetlife that never sleeps

he carries a garbage bag full of statues and hymn books, and cadges cigarettes as regular as a car pulls over to pick up a red skirt

cats play in his sleeve, sparrows nest in his matchbox, he lights his cigarette with a bee

he has become transcendent, transcendent as a whiff of smoke

and his hair eaten away by the streets, his teeth eaten like the windows of derelict buildings, his tongue a swollen carp, his eyes so many murdered tomorrows

he — I recognize him — he walks behind me

Get away! Get away!

COFFEE WITH DOUG

From the window of Finger's Donut Shop,

you and I look out. We sit
in plastic seats, drink cold coffee,
the occasional bite from a day-old donut.

Years ago you had burnt a third eye into your forehead
with a red-hot stone, thinking you were God.
In and out of hospitals, for years sleeping on the
glassed-in veranda of your boarding house —
friends would pray you'd make it through the winter nights.

You start the conversation, talk about the satellite dish across the street,
wonder about those who live below it, whether
they are receptive to the tremors it sends to their subconscious?

We throw pieces of donut to the pigeons in the doorway.
One is pure white. You talk about
childhood, nursing wounded pigeons in an attic room.
You tell me about tiplers and rollers and homing pigeons:
one flies in circles, one somersaults through the air, one carries messages.

I watch the wind through the trees.
In one, it seems to soothe;
in another, it is angry and ravaging.

You point out the maple tree at the corner,
how one day you were stunned to see its green leaves sprinkled with yellow;
it was early summer, and as you stood there,
a wind rifled through the tree, tore every
yellow leaf from its limbs.

We talk about the apartment building down the street
— built in the fifties, already dilapidated —
you point out how they are tarring the roof,
how the metal frame at the roof's edge
looks like a whaler's harpoon, how the orange wheelbarrow
that they are lowering from it, hundreds of feet,
contains the unhatched eggs of tonight's dreams.

HUME CRONYN

Then you tell me how Steve has moved out from your boarding house to live
     with Sharon,
how they leave scraps of meat and bowls of milk in deserted garages,
how they walk on window ledges when they are drunk,
how Steve always carries in his shirt pocket a stone that looks like an ear.

You tell me about the front door that is never used at your place,
about the side door and the eavestrough that was repaired
— how things are looking up for you —
now when it's raining you can enter the side door
without a gush of water soaking you.

And then you mention lunch, you have to be home at noon.
And you return to your cupboard-size room and I, ablaze,
take a streetcar across the city, return to work.

L O V E   P O E M

The Nick Cave look-alike with hair black as gloss paint sitting beside the girl with the studded dog collar around her neck, the young woman in the flower-print dress with three gladiolas lying on her lap, the woman reading a Harlequin romance while her other hand steadies a gold-framed picture of a pit bull wearing a cowboy hat.

It's late at night, we are sitting on a bus, so many single people — only one couple — we are all delirious with the thought of going home alone, the air crackles, we are wrapped in sweat, there's the squeak-squeak of chewing gum, how many times we steal a glance.

And the bus waits in its bay, it waits, its sides are rattling, the smell of worn tires creeps in through the windows, and we wait while the bus driver is down in the subway station licking his fingers dripping from the oozing cinnamon roll that he has just bought.

We sit, the first wave of passengers to board the bus, we sit and watch as the second wave searches for their seats — the man whose tattooed hand grips a Dominion bag stuffed with celery and the cloudy smelling of cheese, the blonde with bare, pearl-white shoulders crossed by satiny black bra straps, the woman in her leopard-skin mini-skirt and velvet cowboy boots, although it's ninety outside,

and the man sitting across from me, with spit-shone penny loafers and a row of pens stuck in the pocket of his Brooks Brothers shirt, according to their height, who sits with all the self-importance of a Bay Street executive,

even he looks at her,

and the bus driver returns with the remainder of his cinnamon roll in a grease-stained paper bag, and the jaggery smell of cinnamon swirls down the aisle of the bus, and it hovers and nudges till our nostrils flare and our skins break out in goose bumps,

and the Carribean woman who sits iconic with the silver hoops of her earrings shimmering, and the Portuguese woman who wears her gold earrings like treble clefs, and I who can't read a word of my book, *The Dynamics of Creation,* we swirl in a sea of sexual currents,

and the seats of the bus, fiberglass and painted with brown squares to resemble cushions, even they, with all the suggestiveness of dirty dish water, are transformed — the tawny brown of lions, one hair of a camel, the pouch of a kangaroo — and on the seat next to me, two pennies sit side by side, and I can not reach over and pick them up.

The bus drives, it drives through the night, past the neo-deco restaurants whose busboys are dragging out bags of garbage, past the 24-hour grocery stores, past the apartment blocks whose closet-size balconies advertize loneliness, into the heart of Lawrence Park,

the bus drives, and we are drawn: the punk girl with her head shaven except for a purple shank of hair that falls across her eyes, the woman in powder-blue socks and Donald Duck sweat-shirt, the man in Jesus sandals and faded T-shirt with dancing figures on it,

we are drawn into the same current, and as each one of us disembarks, all of us singly, except the punk couple, chatting about coming down from an acid trip in the alleyway behind the organic butcher's,

each one of us watches with longing as the bus door clatters open, if only we had the nerve? the courage? the desperation? to ask if the departing person wanted company —

we imagine the walk home/ the shy talk/ the flick of a match to light a cigarette/the extraordinary expectation as keys are pulled from purse or pocket —

the bus door closes with a bang, one less person, and another, and another, till the sexual energy turns to emptiness, exhaustion grows,

and at the first stop after the bridge, the punk couple gets off, and I get off, I speed up and cross the road diagonally so that I don't get stuck behind them on the walk up the hill, I pass the house with the stately blue spruces, pass the house with the driveway of bricks, the house with two ponds,

and as I cross our lawn I notice that the garage door is slightly ajar, there's a sliver of light, it's one of those electric doors, I go to push the buttton but don't because the clattering of the mechanism might wake everyone in the house.

I pull out my keys, see that you've left the front door open, you pick your sleepy self up from the armchair in the living room, say that you've waited up for me, you thought I said I would phone from the subway station and that you'd have gladly picked me up. I said that I hadn't wanted you to wait up for me, I knew you were tired, I'm sorry we got our signals crossed, and anyways, I love the walk in, the houses along Glengowan,

and we sit on the floor of the bedroom, I vacantly stare at the dress you are wearing, it takes me a moment to recognize it, I haven't seen it for years, it's the dress which you wore when I first met you twenty years ago,

blue and cotton and pin-striped and simple with two pockets for your hands and the skewed collar which shows the fragile tent of your collarbone, so delicate your skin, almost transparent, the structure of those bones that will always take me further than any cathedral will,

and I remember our early years of necking in the back seats of cars, the time our bodies smelt inexplicably of oranges, the time two cops on horses knocked on our steamed-up windows at four in the morning, the first time I saw your breasts, the confusion that came over me when I saw three hairs sprouting from one of them,

and we talk about the children asleep in the bedroom, how Blake fell asleep on the living room floor at eight-thirty, how Koy counted up to twenty, about the growing attachment of Chloe and Grandma Teddy to the budgie found on the front lawn, how rare it is that the children fall asleep before we do,

and your legs are drawn up yoga style, your legs are bare, the pink of your underwear shows, your fingers comb through your hair, pushing it off your forehead, then drop to take hold of the hem of your dress — stretched tautly between your knees like an open mouth — pinching it together so that your dress covers your underwear,

then you let go of the hem, mouth opens

I want you so much, twenty years, and I still want you, bursting through my clothes,

through our skins.

DON'T CALL ME A POET

Like the streets of a city it winds through me,
boisterous like children at a playground,
it burns many colours at the end of the street,
it's a piece of newsprint blown in the wind,
the core of an apple fallen in the gutter,
an angel someone has left on the window ledge.

Poetry! For years I wanted to be a poet:
a face like Shelley's, a Byronic club-foot walk would do,
Brechtian glasses that looked inward and outward,
wine-breath of Baudelaire, vatic exclamations of Gregory Corso,
the fantastic trance-like utterances of Robert Desnos.

And then I met people who were poets.
Their nervous hearts were burdened with poetry,
their tongues leaden from gonging too much poetry,
their rectitude — not to be confused with their rectums — stank of rotten
        poetry fish.
Jesus, they even compared their published books to children!
No doubt about it, they held pens that resembled poets' pens,
upgraded to computers that resembled poets' computers,
even raided their dreams and dressed them up as poetry.

Now I no longer want to be a poet
(one must disguise it all costs).
Poetry is something to spear with an umbrella,
something to turn in your hand and pity its fossilized existence, then chuck
        it in the rubbish,
something to put in a taxi for a long ride and when the taxi driver becomes
        suspicious it can't pay he'll thump the daylights out of it,
something to spit apple seeds at,
something to walk across a zebra crossing on Warwick Road, for the trucks
        will never stop for it,
something to wrap in tinfoil and roll down the stairs,
something to push through the window with a rope around its neck,
something to shut in a dirty sock drawer,
something to . . .
BEWARE OF POETRY! IT IS WRITTEN BY POETS!
Call me a street, a child, a piece of rubbish, an apple core, even an angel,
        but don't call me a poet.

II

RINSED SUNSHINE

It's not the fan that opens Apocalypse Now. It's an ordinary fan that whirls around, shooting out shafts of cool air.

I am trying to educate my left hand in the art of Latin American revolutionaries, but my fingernails give away my pedigree.

Nothing has changed. I share my bed with two dolls that the Empress of Festivities donated to me because of my service to the late emperor.

The late emperor was a crook who turned rivers into musty old feathers that not even little boys would pick up to complete their headdresses.

I once read that Geronimo died in an old-age home in Florida at the turn of the century.

If Geronimo died in an old-age home, what are we dying in?

One must live in order to have the aptitude to die, the old emperor once said. But that was in a moment of lucidity before he started to splash eau de Cologne over his mashed bananas.

The dolls have hair the colour of rinsed sunshine. The heat is unmerciful. The rain lasts for several minutes, but dries up almost instantaneously — like drops hitting a hot iron.

I keep the fan on because it sounds like the waves of the ocean. Because it shuts out the sound of TVs on either side of me.

It's not by choice that I stay at this two-storey motel with a french name and a bathtub-sized swimming pool. Money is the deciding factor. Unfortunately, the further one gets from the ocean, the closer one gets to the supermarkets.

On my birthday I went to a restaurant in a well-known hotel. I watched some children play video games in the hallway. One of the games featured a kung-fu master who unleashed a battery of kicks at the faintest flicker of a shadow. The face of the player operating the lever was contorted, as if he was dropping bombs.

I blame my listlessness on the environment. Some environments are overwhelming.

Two dolls to bring life to life. One doll says, Turn off the fan. The other says that the emperor wasn't that bad of a person. And my hand? Why am I reading about Simon Bolivar and José Marti? And why not mention Ché Guevara?

It will soon be midnight. Hunger is eating at me. I get up and count the bananas lying on top of the microwave.

Here's to you Empress, Emperor, Geronimo! I am suffocating in rinsed sunshine.

DESCENT

she belonged to the Guinness family
heiress to millions
she lived in Bloomsbury
a suite in a 5-star hotel

she had a dog
the dog ate steak
slept in her bed
she slept on the floor

when the dog needed a walk
the chauffeur drove it around the square
once when it needed a good stretch
it was driven to Brighton and back

the dog died

many times I saw her walking
an empty dog leash dangling from her hand
at every lamppost she would stop
her thin lips emitting a small hiss

her money dried up
she slept on a bench in Russell Square
her coat once Caribbean blue
now as threadbare as the clouds

I don't know how she managed
everyday a rose in her buttonhole

one night to keep warm
she rolled herself up in a carpet

the carpet had been thrown out by an old lady
the son visiting his mother thought it a shame
(another example of her going potty)
three flights he carried up the carpet
huffing and puffing how heavy it seemed

he unrolled it to show his mother the error of her ways
first petals then the heiress

cold but alive

alive to live for another four months
not found hanging from a dog leash
(the leash lost years back)
not found beneath the wheels of a chauffeur-driven car

she died her face so pale the moon
reflected in her urine puddled at the base of a lamppost

TROLLEY MAN

He has four trolleys strapped together:
Two by two, they form a square.
A broomstick is tied to one of the corners
and a burlap bag flies from it like a flag.
From the sides, a huge drum of cooking oil hangs,
coils of hemp, tin cans, empty bottles of Evian water.
In his four layers of clothes he pushes his trolleys,
a wooden object sticks from the front like a horn,
and overflowing the top — a chair, a plastic box,
a beach umbrella, magazines, a Seven-Eleven paper cup,
all of them kept from tumbling by the glorious wizardry of an extended
     shoelace.

You should see him when he pushes his flotilla down Exhibition Road, turns
     onto Thurloe Street.
Seven bus routes pass through that junction, it's rush hour,
and even though the sky is blue and apple trees are in blossom,
he pushes his flotilla into the haze of sulphuric heaviness,
he pushes his trolleys past the beat-up Austin parked outside the Polish
     restaurant,
past the school children elbowing their way through the straggling bus
     queues,
past the news vendor at the mouth of the South Ken tube station,
around the corner, and down Old Brompton Road.
The sight is magnificent: he could be in Nairobi, Cairo, or Timbuctoo,
and it's always amazed me, I have never heard a car honk at him,
this city handed over to the impetuous car, this city where the pedestrian is
     an obstacle,
this blue-stocking part of London, crammed with Jags and Rolls-Royces,
this part of London, where drivers are as puffed up as their cars.

I've seen him, when the rain is spilling down and the windshield wipers of
     passing cars are frantically swishing back and forth,
I've seen him camped in front of the derelict lot which once was the Iranian
     embassy,
the sheets that cover his trolleys battoned down, the tarpaulin that he's
     huddled beneath, billowing, as if he was sailing into the eye of a storm,
and he, impassive, stripping chicken from a bone, or drinking coffee,

or, one time, I swear he was counting the raindrops so he could pass through
        to the other side.

Often he is by the derelict lot, but on the nicest days of the summer,
he parks himself on one of the corners of Thurloe Square,
an arm's length from a house that rents at a quarter of a million a year.
Inside the maidservant is riding the elevator with a glass of ice-water,
while he, sitting under an umbrella that extends from one of the trolleys,
looks as if he has just finished the most extravagant of dinners.
He sits on a stool perusing a book as thick as a volume of an encyclopedia:
why do I think that the book is written in some ancient language that built
        the pyramids or thundered like the falls of Victoria?

Where does this man come from?
Kadanga village? The Niger delta? Mozambique? Or some impossibly
        crowded African city?
Sometimes he talks to himself, solemn and sonorous.
Once when I was crossing the street with the children
and stepped back in alarm, because I had almost walked the four of us into
        an oncoming car,
he laughed, not malicious, but a good-natured laugh revelling in the
        predominance of the car.
How many times have I walked past him?
Why have I never spoken to him?
How does he sleep? Where does he piss?
Where does he get his food (I've never seen him beg)?

And again I pass him: the sun has dropped behind the white crown of the
        Victoria and Albert.
What is that look on his face?
How many continents has he crossed?
What happened to the loved ones in his life?
One feels that something has broken in him, so deep this brokeness,
like travelling into Death Valley, irradiated for 25,000 years,
there's no mending, only that spark which refuses to be extinguished.

You and I load up our trolleys, bring home enough food for a week;
he loads up his trolleys, pushes them from one site to another.
What journey is he preparing for, loaded up with all our discarded objects?
Today I see him, and instead of turning away, he looks at me.
Will I stop? Does it matter if I have nothing to say, little to give?

I worry about intruding; I worry about how we abandon people.
He sits and smoothes out the pages of a wet book.
A poster, advertizing cosmetics, hangs from his trolleys.
I pass by, helplessness weighs in the pit of my stomach.

WORD FUN(D)
(After Paul Eluard)

If a man sneaks up behind you and shouts celery
You know that he's talking about the puddle
Nibbling at your toes

If a man shouts lard
You know he's talking about the rain
Of pineneedles and how they stick
In your hair

If he shouts menstrual cycle
You know the seasons have donned their cloaks
And are scaring the daylights out of obtuse
Pumpkins

If he shouts virus
You know that a swarm of bees has eaten up all
The candles in your drawers

If he shouts lethargy
You know the sky is panting
And about to turn out its pockets
Of dust

If he shouts rhumba
Fingers are sticky with a bluish liqueur
Squeezed from oblong oranges

If he shouts loganberry
There are few ways to suppress the violence of panic
That springs from the soles of your feet
And sweeps in eddies to the
Crown of your scalp

If he shouts mouth
You know that a window has fallen from the top
Floor of a skyscraper
Is a millisecond from hitting the ground

Shame
The stars are hiding behind the clouds
Naked except for their pointed shoes

Rambunctious
The last colour discovered in the colour spectrum

France
The name of an extinct alligator

Abbatoir
A vegetable patch which flourishes without
A spot of sunshine

If he shouts God Bless You
You know he's talking about rotting fish
And your sanctimonious
Correctness

Something to Do with the Stars & the Beautiful Unseating of a Cop

I met you twenty years ago in the back seat of a car, it was permeated with the smell of a horse's mouth which, pressed up against the window, could not stand the idea that we were floating, & when the cop, sitting on the horse like a bottle with no neck, tapped the window with his blackjack, your sweater squeezed in the corner of the back seat unravelled & we lifted our hands to plead with the horse, jealousy would get him nowhere &, anyway, that piece of junk sitting on him, hijacking our transparency, he deserved to be hurled into the river which flowed past the nose of our car, problem is he'd probably dissolve like a donut dunked in piping hot coffee & fowl up the river with his stinking crippledom, poor, poor soul, for him there was not a star in the sky, we had swallowed several hundred stars & didn't even need a Bromo, & flowers will never have a monopoly on beauty, for we were comets & several other things beside that, while this cop mounted on his horse, stinking of chicken & amphetamines & chewing on his tongue for sustenance — words cannot be squeezed from a stone — oh poor, poor soul could not even remember that long lost feeling that once transported him, & I never had a flicker of a thought whether we could sustain this night for a week, a month, a lifetime, that's the nature of youth, but the horse was so old & dreamed that he was a pile of feathers, he was tired of gulping down nuts and bolts for nourishment & every-thing else that holds a cop together, so he gave up the ghost & the cop floun-dered muddily in the puddle in which our rear tire nestled, the stench was so bad that we emptied our ashtrays & ate a half dozen daffodils, we swore we would never again park next to the police stables, everyone knows that cops can't sleep at night, but who would've ever thought that they kept their horses up, too, so we drove across the bridge & found another parking spot, there were still a lot more stars to swallow.

So, the Question

Once
when we were eighteen
your parents went to Florida
you smuggled me into your house
and although you went to the odd class
for a week we were tied to your bed
We would dress up for sex
undress for sex
and once you wore nothing but an apron
how beautiful what you served
and when your parents returned their house was never the same
the smell of the sea, tropical jungles and fantastic mosses
crept into their shoes and staleness and tiny pieces of buttered
        bread.

Now
we neither dress nor undress
we pull up night shirts
it's over in a few minutes
we're so tired, mustn't wake the children who sleep in the same room
        with us
we whisper how the children are doing at school
the rent is due tomorrow, Chloe's ballet test the day after, who will
        do the shopping
and minutes later we fall into a sexless sleep
a tear moistening the corner of our pillows.

I will
always believe that sex
is more mysterious than the moon and the tides
more delicate than the rain
more ample than Noah's Ark
more expansive than seven continents
more holy
than the bell tolling at the bottom of the sea
So, the question —
how can we escape these nights of crust?

OUR FLAT

Our flat lives on the fourth floor
not high enough to talk to the sky
but low enough to shake from the trains
& turn hazy from the buses

Height is no protection
dust accumulates paint peels cracks grow
we never dust
cracks are covered with children's art
& what is peeling paint
but walls breaking into flower

A knitting machine hangs above the fireplace
an umbrella handle its tail
a bicycle fender its head
it's our pet bird
his pocket-watch eye peers at us
afraid we'll plunder his nest of matches

Who's that at the door
it's our friend Stephen
he wants to pass through the roof hatch
for a whiff of Hyde Park air
& a wink from the dome of the V&A

One of the children is playing in the closet
he's dragged out his potty
one has climbed into the dryer
one's trimming the hairs of the violin bow
one's wrapping her doll in my jogging pants

Clothes hang from door knobs
shoes live under chairs
books take root in a stack of orange crates
(ho! the fragrance of words is everywhere)
the bath tub is alive with silverfish
a caterpillar pokes its head from the toy box

The bedroom is filled with ladders
children jump from bunk to bunk
so many dreams we have to open the window
pillows fly through the air
another clock bites the dust
time changes colour sometimes stands still

Who are we
sometimes anger lots of love birthday cakes
the children outgrow their shoes at an alarming rate
an aimless day is a priceless gift
& when the rain grows lonely
the roof opens up with its many holes

BROKEN

He was down on his hands and knees.
As if he'd urinated, the pavement
was a wet stream.
He was down,
his mouth to the pavement,
he was licking it up,
licking up the wetness,
his lips were bleeding,
bleeding, two spots on his lower lip,
bleeding, two stars,
bleeding.
He raised his head,
raised his arms to the sky,
he was shouting,
his fists clenched,
spittle in his beard,
words were swallowed up by the sky,
people passed by,
words were swallowed,
people passed,
a woman said, disgusting,
a man hurried by with his daughter,
turned his body to shelter her.
Down he went again,
greedily drinking up the pavement,
lips bleeding,
bleeding, two stars,
bleeding,
sucking up the wetness,
moving from side to side,
moving,
streaking the pavement,
streaking it with
blood.

Behind him a broken bottle,
fallen from his pocket, fallen,
smashed to tiny pieces.
Behind him, his broken bottle.

CARLOS

he jumped from the bridge
thirty feet he jumped
several witnesses saw him
two saw him struggling at the parapet
saw him struggling with a black figure
a figure with two black horns
they saw him struggling
he jumped he was pushed
he jumped he was pushed
he'd bought a new suit that day
wore his new suit hit the highway
a car ploughed into him he flew up
was hit by another car
dragged hundreds of feet

no more demented deliveries
no more paranoid ravings
he would stand outside the donut shop
shout at those who passed by
you mental junkie CIA fucked-up pricks
you boot-licking cock-sucking retards
he'd only shout when he thought a person was weaker than himself
or would take pity on him
sometimes he misjudged
would be punched to a pulp
would lie in his blood
oh Lord what has happened to us
would lie in his blood
no one no one no one
would call an ambulance

he was from Sudbury
graduated from high school
was an honor student
dropped out of university
found work at a mountain resort
worked up to second chef
but he couldn't escape

escape from the crack in the wooden ladle
the crack like forked lightning
with his right hand he held on
with his left hand he walked into the blizzard
nothing was written on the snow
nothing could be found
to still the little man sitting in his ear
whispering concoctions of fortunes
insinuating fortunes
charred fortunes
knife-sharp fortunes

he fled from the snow
sought refuge in a valley of orchards
thought picking apples would be safer
but voices whispered
whispered Eve's apples Eve
he drowned his evenings
began to drown his days
when he lay down
the devil was hatched
Carlos was no match
more and more dope
it didn't vanquish the devil
but it kept him in the next room
the next room threatening to crash through
crash through like Goya's Saturn

he once belonged to a family
his father thought he was too big for his britches
his brothers thought he was too small
for them the life of the hands was everything
brick dust was everywhere
God was three square meals
his mother idolized him
saved money dreamed of a graduation gown
but he heard the lash of whips in the wind
the moon on his bedroom floor was a kiss
the lash of a kiss the kiss of a whip

he crossed the country to a cockroached room in Parkdale
the night was filled with eyes
the CIA lived in his floorboards
the radio stole his voice
his secret research
he was the illegitimate son of Gloria Swanson
he was the Messiah
he would save the world from Rockefeller
thousands of pages
he could not trust the locks on his trunk
thousands of pages consigned to the tundras of his memory
his memory burned like cigarette ends
the only end was when was he going to end
his eyes burned like the thick bottom of bottles filled with kerosene
his heart was a spent torrent of words
chewed like a hunk of tongue
he jumped he was pushed
he jumped he was pushed
oh da-daa-daaa oh ma-maa-maaaaa

his mother had moved back to Portugal years ago
was in Toronto at the time
had come back to look for him
look for Carlos her very own Carlos
where was Carlos where
he jumped he was pushed
he jumped he was pushed
the end of his stay in boarding house rooms
the end of stench-air gabbing dust
the end of so many hatreds
(so many people who hated)
the end of Saturn crashing through the wall
of years of hateful sex
of years of no sex
of worms of apples
the sermons got too loud
the end the end

the last time his brother saw him
Carlos had apple blossoms in his hair
it was midnight

he was shouting
he woke up the kids
woke up the neighbours
his brother was too scared to let him in
he jumped he was pushed
he jumped he was pushed

Born to Buy

Buy a pair of rubber gloves to save your hands while your life rots at the
  centre;
Buy the Nike revolution to run through the day at extra speed while your
  soul is craving to be absolutely still;
Buy a V.C.R. to fill your evening with comedy while the day grows black with
  threat;
Buy Joy and dab your body with voluble fragrances to engage your man
  while your mouth is dry with no words;
Buy a bottle of wine to relax, and a case of beer to throttle the boredom,
  while the wind is slowly eating up your garden;
Buy a Lear jet to guarantee your timely presence at business meetings while
  your children fly in the untimely kingdom of glue;
Buy a home computer to fill your free time with space games while the earth
  is working up a devastating hunger;
Buy a Mercedes-Benz to reward your easy-won successes while increasing
  neighbourhoods are beating empty spoons;
Buy a tube of champagne toothpaste to break the sterile Christmas holiday
  with a laugh while millions of children are toothless in their crawl to the
  grave;
Buy an armful of newspapers to keep up with thirty different wars while
  entire countries are cut down;
Buy a greenhouse upbringing for your children — don't tell them about
  bombs and wars and poverty — while all around is crumbling because
  of the wholesale marketing of ignorance;
Buy a fancy aquarium to relax your shot nerves, and populate it with exotic
  fish to simulate the rainbow, while the sky is so murky it can no longer
  be seen;
Buy a Sony Trinitron for your kitchen to pass the hours of cooking away while
  your food grows as glossy and plastic as your favourite soap opera;
Buy a sunny condominium in sunny Florida to rest your retired bones, ride
  the tranquilized slopes of nostalgia, coast on gin fizzes, obliterate
  whatever wisdom you've gained from experience, while the universal
  heart grows as watery as iceberg lettuce;
BUY! BUY! and BUY!
And when you're exhausted from buying, take a rest and buy a holiday: the
  further you travel from home, the more likely you will come across a
  purchase that will excite your weary attention, and once again you are
  on the recovery path to feverish buying.
BUY! BUY! and BUY!

TWO LIVES

I'm reading *On the Road* & for weeks I've been reading the Beats,
I come stumbling out of a café, its easy chairs so moth-eaten that I often
      disappear into the world of rusted springs, plaster craniums are
      mounted on the wall with price tags dangling from their frontal lobes,
      & everyone in the place is at least twenty years younger than me,
On the Road is playing havoc with my brain cells: all the characters wanting
      their lives to flare up & like fabulous roman candles spider "the holy
      void of uncreated emptiness,"
the two heroes of the book, Dean Moriarty & Sal Paradise, hotrodding one
      automobile after another to locate that saintly tenor sax blowing the
      lid off that small cave we call life & trying to understand more than can
      be understood, while a waiter called Lampshade deposits one drink
      after another on the wine & whiskey-soaked tables,
I come stumbling out, walk through Soho Park — seeing the weather-beaten
      statue of Charles II, I want to mount its nibbled pedestal & devour the
      grammar of this lunch-hour space: latex-clad couriers fondling their
      bicycles, crazed procession of bongo-thumping Hare Krishnas, lonely
      Italian girls pining for blue skies, lolling prostitutes blotting out end-
      less evenings, sad-eyed winos sucking out of paper bags, displaced
      Geordies thumbing through medical texts,
I stumble through a puddle & soak my shoes, if I could lie down & be water,
even the pigeons, who I've never had any sympathy for, if I could nobble
      about on their orange bandy legs miraculously avoiding the cracks in
      the paving stones,
crossing Oxford Street, a spanking-new post office van almost runs me over,
      if I could run over myself & be resurrected.
in front of the redbrick Abbey National, a young woman is crying, her pimp
      pulling out crisp bills from a cash machine, her body craving, I'm
      craving — what mask am I wearing?
I pass a young man sitting in a doorway, he could be a Bodhisattva sitting
      on the banks of the Ganges, behind him his mate sleeps on milk
      crates & cardboard,
I'm heading for a place tucked between a Greek & Indian restaurant, wafer
      thin & five tables, it's painted refuge blue,
stepping off the curb, bloody hell if the same post office van doesn't come
      careening around the corner & almost run me down again,
ghostly with gyprock dust, two workmen sprawl in chairs outside of an
      Alpine-looking sandwich shop with the un-Alpine name, Munchies,

a woman passes me, beret pulled down over her forehead, dragging on a
      cigarette as if she was a hungry animal & it was the only sage in the
      desert,
I come to my haven, I've been saving it up for months for a moment like this,
      I reel back when I read the prices, the woman behind the bar dressed
      in wake-up yellow,
I keep walking, muttering to myself, wait at the corner as traffic hurtles by,
      a woman, with Violent Daffodils stamped across the back of her
      leather jacket, is telling her boyfriend to brush the egg from his lips,
I dash across the street, the wind blustering spits of rain, & by the park
      which only opens for the summer months (what! don't we need parks
      more than ever during the winter?), a man with a patch on his eye is
      picking up twigs from the pavement,
a stately black man asks me where New Bedford Way is — some library or
      other — but I can only get him halfway there,
an old Italian passes me, pursing his lips as if he was trying to remember
      how to whistle (why at age five is learning to whistle & snapping one's
      fingers the most important thing in life?),
I descend into the basement of a medical building, hungry for a fishcake &
      maybe run into Chris, yak about poetry, but the lineup is too long & I
      flee from university students discussing their 45-year-old fathers &
      overheated libraries,
I scoot in the back of the British Museum, they're checking bags for bombs,
      I'm a primary candidate for I have a library of Beat books on my back
      & no telling when I'm going to explode,
once in the library, I find that my usual seat is occupied by a grey-haired
      eminence gloating over my displacement,
I plonk myself down in the next aisle, leaf through the blue-covered tomes of
      the Dictionary of Literary Biography till I come to Harold Norse, the
      first words I read — "The cardinal sin is boredom,"
I pack up my books & rush home, frantically I search through several
      months of Sunday papers to find two coupons which I staple to an
      application form for a £50 flight to any one of twelve destinations in
      Europe,
the mad dash to the post office, if I catch the 3:30 mail, it may arrive in time
      to qualify, the lineup at the post office stretches to the door & outside
      — twice the confounding manifestations of British organizational skills —
      I buy stamps from a machine in the wall,
I'm at full tilt by the time I hit Blake's hotel, I pass behind it, a mews which
      is a veritable parking lot of BMWs, I laugh as I watch myself striding
      down the street — why am I only wearing one glove?

for once I'm early for picking up the kids from school, my daughter has a
      netball match on the other side of Holland Park, we bum a ride from a
      friend, my sons expressing whoops of delight since it's the first time
      they've rode in a Jeep,
we drive through sidestreets — St. Ann's, Wilsham, Sirdar — arrive in time
      for the rain & the netball match in which my daughter spends more
      time covering one of her teammates than the forward of the opposing
      team & with wet shoulders and red faces, the only reward they reap
      from their loss is a packet of stale crisps,
we bum a ride from another friend, once home I cook chicken & rice for
      dinner — dishes to wash, clothes to wash in a machine that only
      works if the knob is turned manually for each cycle,
the children do their homework, practice reciting poems for tomorrow's
      competition, one types up information about Siberian tigers & draws
      the most beautiful tiger stalking through a landscape of bushy trees,
I lug two brimming bags of bottles & papers to the recycling bins, carry on
      to the gym, where Christos, knowing my weakness for obituaries &
      Burmese politics, stuffs three newspapers into my hands,
wet-haired, I return home, throw the laundry into the dryer & gulp down two
      glasses of apple juice while listening to E-Bow The Letter, which still
      moves me after two weeks of listening,
close to midnight, I think about Sal Paradise's amazing hope that he & Dean
      Moriarty will someday live on the same street with their families &
      grow to be a couple of oldtimers together, I ghostly float through the
      flat checking to see if the heaters are off & taps not dripping,
finally I flop into bed, of course I can't sleep! how can I hold this life in one
      body?
then a more optimistic mood rises in me, I quietly laugh — two lives is
      better than one, will I ever be able to unite them? have I united them?
      does it really matter? & life, being short, two lives isn't enough.

III

PARKING

We sat in the back seat of the Roadmaster
The seat sticky from a spilt milkshake
We had smoked so many cigarettes
The ashtray foamed like an epileptic

I held you in my arms
You showed me the blood
That welled up on your ring finger
A dog was pawing at the window

We had swallowed so much of each other
That the stale music from the radio
And the hiss from the punctured tire
Caressed us like gun powder

A horse came prancing down the road
An ant crawled over the rear-view mirror
I pulled out my change purse
Was full of stories and late thoughts

You stroked my cheek and laughed
Asked about the dog: Should we feed it
The horse was the colour of chestnuts
Was licking our headlights like sugar

I got stuck on one of my stories
You clung to me as never before
Your hair was angel's hair
The smell of freshly-fallen rain

You said: Who cares if our tire is punctured
Who cares if the dog is pawing at our window
The horse licking our headlights
Who cares if you stop in the middle of a story

And I didn't care
I didn't care if my change purse fell
If our cigarettes burnt holes in the upholstery
You were somewhere no one else had ever been

MY UNCLE

The man who built a boat
in his basement
and can't get it out
is my uncle.

The mast goes up through
a hole in the kitchen floor
and when it grows hot
he hoists up the sail.

He spends a great deal
of time with us children.
The sail, as blue as his eyes:
on it we have painted

the great white whale,
the marble-looking sea cow,
penguins on an ice floe,
the solemn wisdom of a pelican.

My uncle only goes out at night.
He collects stones from the beach —
his father stone, his laughing stone,
a stone that is from the centre of the earth.

He finds the worn-down necks of bottles
and wears them as rings.
He shapes a sky out of driftwood,
a lighthouse out of matches.

My uncle sings songs like the waves of the sea.
He keeps them in a barrel of sand
which he sieves through his fingers
when we sleep in the hull of his boat.

He tells stories from every part of the world.
He has known the tribes of the Congo basin,
the sailors of Patagonia, the Eskimos of Greenland,
the dancers of Kapuskasing, the divers of Senegal.

With my uncle we cry from sadness.
He has made us feel the smallest loss.
We breathe the breath of others,
feel their happiness as if our own.

One moment my uncle can talk
until we are laughing with tears.
Other times he says nothing
as if he is living inside himself.

My uncle is always eating fruit:
fruit that you peel, fruit that you slice,
fruit that you bite into with no preparation,
fruit that tickles and puckers the mouth.

There are times when he looks into mirrors
as if they were windows;
looks into windows
as if they were mirrors.

My uncle loves to hold us.
He needs us like we need him,
and sometimes even the distance
of air is too much.

My uncle is sailing with us.
He lets us take the rudder.
We seem to be nowhere, but he can smell
the dew on the grass.

We get out the ropes.
We are near; but not so near
that we can't throw out a bottle with a message —
'Be home soon, but not today.'

MONDAY NIGHT AT THE TROUBADOUR

You are in a small room in the basement of a coffee house.
The room is cluttered with a crowd of beaten-up church pews.
You follow the crack in the floor which runs like a lightning bolt.
Cigarette smoke rolls up and hangs in billowing clouds
(only the flies have the good sense to choke on it).
There is a poet reading.
The stage is not a stage but a continuation of the scrabbled floor
(as it should be and never is: for no one should be raised above others, even
        by an inch).
On the door there is a metal sign: Applicants for employment in this
        establishment should apply at the Labour Exchange.
The door is bolted. To get in you stick your hand through the letterbox to
        signal your presence.

There is a poet reading.
Unlike most of the poets who bring their poems in plastic bags,
unlike most of the poets who take several minutes to locate the poem they
        wish to read
(and if they don't locate it, it is always understood that the poem they are
        reading is inferior to the one they were going to read)
he pulls his poem from his coat pocket.
The poet reading, he's a mathematician,
the moths have eaten his sweater, evicted from his bedsit the harsh words
        of his landlord chase him like bees, he clings to the Johny Walker in
        his pocket,
usually his stream-of-consciousness poems shut down attention after several
        lines,
but tonight it is a long poem about the death of his mother,
and it sings, it weeps, she sits in the tree of our eyes with her violin hands, her
        heart of bitter hair,
and the chatter of poets, standing at the back of the room, swapping stories
        about poems that were written and not written,
and the poet who organizes, just back from the Himalayas, with snow on his
        shoulders, who will preside over these Monday night rituals for the next
        ten years, who is always studying his list and tapping the shoulder of
        the next poet to read,
and the cigarette ash that is falling to the ground,
and the flies that are choking,
all are listening to his words, so sweet, so lyrical, so beautiful,

and a small fire runs up the spine, tingles the hair,
and the list is forgotten, no one is tapped on the shoulder,
there is no longer the need to chatter about unwritten poems,
the ashes pile up like ancient cairns,
and the church pews float like arks upon the holy flood.
The poem ends. There is a hush, then a wave of clapping.

And the poet that follows,
he writes about a woman he met in the seventh house of the seventh month,
he writes about her hair that harbours a thousand oyster-coloured sails,
he writes about her eyes dark as the last swig of a bottle of red wine,
he writes about the fragile tent of her collarbone, the cool brass of her
        cheekbones,
he writes, he writes about her,
he has left his plastic bags at home,
from memory he reads his poems —
no pieces of paper, no hand-written words needing a stumbling pause to
        decipher, no pages missing,
nothing between his words and the audience.

And the poet after him,
in his pin-striped suit, looking as if he'd just rushed from the City,
except that his hair corkscrews in wild illumination, his suit crumpled with
        volcanic articulation,
he has tramped from the blue-domed reading room of the British Museum,
has just completed a manuscript on the history of penal reform in England,
in his poems he writes about a young man dying in the darkness of a
        Kensington studio flat,
about a 55-year-old builder on the dole whose heart is popping out of his
        chest from nothing to do,
about a hooker whose face was ripped open by a broken bottle because she
        was holding someone else's baby.

And the poet after him,
only seventeen, he jumps around the stage,
he spits out his poems as if each one was an ambulance hurtling down a
        mountain,
he sparks like a flag pole on fire, he spits and sparks:
where Moses is a national liberation fighter who could never be contained in
        ten commandments, let alone sixty-nine,
where the chosen few do not sleep through their dreams,

where the music of church bells is ripened in cellars,
where walnut prophecy erupts from the magnetic offering of seven silences.

And the poet after him,
just back from an associate-professorship at Princeton,
in one hand he holds Anna, in the other Nazim,
he is only six months away from a jump out of a third-storey window,
all the poets from Russia to Turkey cannot construct a parachute to break his
        fall and the imploding sound of fifty-seven bones,
he reads a poem about his twin who lives under a bridge with a snowflake, who
        carries the French countryside in an antipodean knapsack,
who conspires with Henry Miller and cries through the vatic telephone that
        measures the all too much shoe of life.

And the poet after,
she stands on a chair and sings her poems,
her glimmering, henna-coloured hair, the white mask of her face,
her enormous red smock covered with buttons of every imaginable size and
        colour,
she writes about the ideological eyebrows of politically correct Dadaists,
a thin sentence which wraps around her waist like a boa constrictor,
a marching band that plays drums the colour of her sex,
a forty-eight hour poem that is a staircase to her dreams.

And the poet after,
with the sturdy body of a whaler, eyes as stricken as a wounded whale,
his poems are so lonesome, so bleak, so filled with the instruments of
        psychiatric terror,
poem by poem he claims back the little pieces of himself that stumbled and
        ended up in files:
files that extol the hallucinated barbarism of electric shock treatment,
files that contain all the nourishing succor of a glacial onslaught.

And the one after,
her black hair tied back in a knot, her eyes as green as bay leaves,
so shy, she disappears behind the black curtain pulled across the door-sized
        hole in the wall,
disappears into a cavern behind the stage and shouts out her poem,
a poem with a page-long title, a poem in which the first word still lurks in
        irretrievable darkness,
a poem in which she comes to a stumbling halt.

This is the end of the evening,
and you file upstairs through the kitchen steaming with odours of parsley
     and soup and omelettes,
you walk beneath the beam with its hanging pots and the Indian chief that
     leans precariously from above,
you push through the oaken door carved with its procession of cherub-faced
     musicians: some tramp to the late-night bar, some take the 74 bus to
     Hackney, some make their way south of the river, one to a building that
     shakes every time the tube pulls into the station, one to Shalford House
     which seems to be dreamt by the torched car in the parking lot, one
     who cannot sleep and walks all-night long.
The end. There is no ending, but the approaching morning brings you one day
     closer to next Monday.

Sing Man Sing

blue   beaten up   black eye
i carry blood in my pocket
grey sweat drips from my body
the snow invites me

i was told to sing
sing man sing
sing if you know what's good for you

jail   i was in jail
we were watching tv
the stink of the john
i carried the slut of my body around   whose
body was it   my mind was a tight handkerchief
sing man sing

i looked at those who were ordering me to sing
(if i didn't sing i'd get the shit beaten out of me)
and i looked at those who were watching tv
(if i did sing i'd get the shit beaten out of me)

sing if you know what's good for you

and those who were watching tv
were bigger than those who
were ordering me to sing

so i didn't sing

and i got the shit beaten out of me
but the damage wasn't as great

one day i'll get out of here
some asshole social worker
will tell me i have a choice
a good kick in the rear
and i can have a better life

let me tell you something
when you're down
when you're down and
poverty sticks in the throat
like a fist

there is only one choice
sing man sing
there is only one choice
and that is between the lesser of two
beatings

one landlord fucks you
another comes at you with a gun
one roommate jabbers all night
another picks you clean
your cheque is enough for rent
but not for food
is enough for food
but not for rent

at least in jail
you can size up who
is larger and who is smaller

outside   you can't tell

like a magnet you're drawn
to the larger beating

the fist of poverty
i carry blood in my pocket
i walk around with black-eyed jail
burning sweat   the snow invites

BIRTHDAY POEM

Friends gathered for my birthday.

One pulled off his boots
And talked continuously about his feet.

A woman, who I was told had committed suicide,
Gave me a kiss, but it could not reconstitute the years.

Why was my sister hiding behind the curtains?
She was giving such a beautiful rendition of an Armenian legend.

My oldest friend came in carrying my childhood attic on his back;
He said next year he would bring the ladder.

Who was that over in the corner shaving his head?
He mixed his hair with fish scales and presented it like a flower.

An old girlfriend gave me a plate full of sand
And left me with the imprint of her hand.

Walt Whitman dropped in for a minute,
Chided me for my immature efforts to imitate him.

My wife promised to read one of my poems
But fell asleep on the second word.

My children crossed the room carrying the biggest sunflower I'd ever seen.
They dropped it at my feet like a log.

I cut into what looked like my least favorite fruit, a watermelon,
was delighted to discover it was Black Forest cake.

My old teacher of business sat over in the corner.
He opened his hands and gave me an exquisitely delicate cobweb.

My uncle, who'd lost his leg making a film with Werner Herzog,
Stumped around the house pretending he was a cloud.

My niece sat under the kitchen table, illustrating an envelope.
Inside was a voucher for a free lesson in sky-diving.

My Grandfather came specially from his stay in the grave,
Gave me a snail and a conversation which lives at the bottom of the sea.

Where was my mother? She was upstairs wrapping my present.
Why didn't she know that some presents can't be wrapped?

And who's that with a pumpkin in her hand —
My grade six teacher singing a Christmas carol I'd completely forgotten.

I hate birthdays, I haven't celebrated one in twenty years,
but if nothing is risked, I'll never have a party like this.

HANDFUL OF TRUTHS

The snake has woven my shirt.

Who said that all oceans are made up of water?
I have seen a man howl like the ocean
and be as dry as the sand.

I have seen a road that burned like a rose
and all men who followed it drown like a stone.

A leaf may float on the wind
but the tree is never the same.

The sky can turn monstrous with clouds
while a kernel of corn still shines like the sun.

A word can open you like a flower
and be sharper than a knife.

Men who fall down and kiss the earth
know the long journey to a woman.

Even if the world were draped in black,
the sight of an ant is a miracle.

Who can forget a tree late at night
when the leaves swim like a shoal of fish.

Whoever finds a starfish
is married to the rope of heaven.

There is no ending.
Tomorrow arrives with a dose of oblivion

or another handful of truths.

GREEN WHERE ARE YOU

i'm a tourist in this country

i sit across from an old man
he sits in a wheelchair
he stares in front of himself sees nothing
large rheumy eyes
he sits with his wife
she scratches her head
every time she scratches
raven-black her wig shifts
they sit at a table
she takes hold of his wheelchair
moves him closer to the table
moves him closer to her
he stares out blankly
stares like a burnt-out lightbulb
the coffee is hot
he takes it in his two hands
she helps him lift it to his lips
he drinks it is too hot
he drinks it scalds his throat
he drinks
he is still holding it
she is still holding it
they lower it to the table
he speaks she speaks
words one word two words
a sentence is too lavish

three thousand miles from home
this country of sun and cheap breakfasts
i'm sitting in a shopping mall
with my children
in the food area
at a table
america you think of everything
a table with a duplo board to keep the kids busy
mine are building a house
frantically building

alternating the colours
first red then blue
then green
everywhere they look for green
green they shout green
green where are you

next to us a young couple
she has sun-bleached hair
she is always moving her head
her hair swings like the rope of a bell
it swings and there's always a smile on her face
it swings
and his hair is always falling across his eyes
falling he pushes it off his forehead
he has a rat-tail
a rat-tail braided with colour
she is talking about Liz who she was supposed to meet an hour ago
talking about what her mother wants for Christmas
how that boy walking by looks like River Phoenix
how new her new sweater is

the children are knocking down the house
the pieces are bouncing off the floor
bouncing red and green
blue and yellow
bouncing off the floor

the old couple stare in front of themselves
sometimes they look at one another
once or twice he looks over at me
once or twice his eyes lose that blank look
she picks up his coffee cup
she holds it to his lips
tips it how does she guage how much to tip it
once he gulps panic in his eyes
coffee dribbles down his chin
few words
I'm dying for them just once just once to smile at one another
just the faintest smile

the young couple she's laughing
don't john don't
he's reached into his seven-up
ice-cubes in his hand
he hovers ice-cubes in his hand
don't john don't
he stuffs them down her front
she laughs she shakes her sweater
ice-cubes come tumbling out
one is caught she laughs
she reaches down dislodges it
she laughs they laugh

the old man he picks up his coffee
he shakes his head
his cup follows an upward path
jerkily jerkily
she watches she watches
the cup touches his lip
trembling hand
he tips it

my children are under the table
under the table
looking for yellow
looking for red

he looks at me once more
i could cry could
am crying
why don't i know this man
he could be my father
where is his family
is he only interested in death
i've never believed in prince andrei's death scene
life will always be more interesting than death
(except when the young abandon the old)
if i could give him one year of my life
would i

i'm a tourist here

DOUG REVISITED

He pulled out a kidney-shaped stone
from behind his ear:
it was to ward off
evil spirits

In his beard
there were no breadcrumbs
or saliva
like pearls
only the flow of wiry
brown rivers

He told me his mother
had recently visited him
she was 84
lived in paradise
she took him out to lunch
where they drank beer
& ate hamburgers

We were in the basement
of his boarding house
the walls were sweating
it was early evening
but no one
made a move to turn on
the lights

We sat on a red couch
with tar-like blotches on it
an archaic tv
stood against the far wall
a man reclining on the other couch
got up to turn on the tv
but a woman in the corner
began to howl

From a quiver
that hung from his neck
Doug removed a pencil
and scribbled
on the inside of a cigarette package:
emotional tilt
     (when disturbed)
     BUILD!
build up your mind

The telephone rang
continued to ring
a pay telephone
that looked as if it'd been ripped
off the wall several times
the man reclining on the couch
continued to watch us with
one eye
I told Doug I was
surprised he was
still up
in heat like this
he used to go to bed
in the afternoon
sleep 16 hours

He laughed & said
that's all they do here
SLEEP/SLEEP/SLEEP
he now went to bed at nine
he showed me a number '6'
brass & polished
no larger than a thumbnail
these are six off-duty angels he said
who come to the rescue of the seventh
when the demons of sleep
threaten

There was a sound of wings
a boy flew into the room
DINNER he shouted

then turning a circle
he sped out
I was flabbergasted by this burst of life
asked Doug where the boy
came from

He warned me it was 5 more years
till the apocalypse
the world would be flooded
great ships would come down
& he'd return to heaven
when the water subsided
the earth would be purified
a new civilization would begin
he would not return
for another 8000 years
his work was in heaven
the boy's work was here
he was the cook's son

Meanwhile Doug had to attend
to dinner
he stood up offered his hand
I thought of how I was born the same year
& in the same hospital as him
I who was returning to a rented house
a wife & three children
he to 8000 years of heaven
what a strange but necessary
friendship

A Night In

I sit across from you

on the table
a knife, and an apple

I have always loved
my apples without the skin

you have always loved
playing with the peeled skins
prodding them with the knife

I want to talk about
mystic flights,
a Tibetan monk
who torched himself,
Tolstoy at Astapovo

you want to talk about
a broken step
that needs repairing,
the wind beating at the window,
the loneliness of your mother

and I bite into white mooniness,
my eyes fixed on the sleeve
of your blouse

and you poke at the skin,
bury it in the white sugar

not a word is said

A Day at the Cottage

What sort of day is it
when it is dominated by visits to
two supermarkets: one to buy FREE TIDE
which was not *free*
but free from phosphates;
the other to buy fish to barbecue
though I forgot to buy
the coals.

In between the supermarkets,
I dumped a bulging bag of laundry
into two washing machines
at the laundromat,
went to Canadian Tire to buy a bug house
for my son,
and before hitting the second supermarket
stuffed the clothes into two dryers
and plugged them each
with four quarters.

It is true,
in the morning I had swum
with the children
and all of us had jumped off the big rock
plunging into the water
with white splashing.

But it was more
that I had wanted —
it was a day of breezes,
but cooking for seven people
I had no time
to be wrapped in the breezes
and whisper to the moss
restless songs
that are forever bubbling.

And when I went to bed,
she who I love,
she who had almost fallen
asleep at the wheel
while driving for ice-cream cones,
she fell asleep
before I could touch her,
and although I can hear
the wind in the leaves,
inside here, it's still and sweaty,
and I feel pulverized
like the skin of the blueberry
caught in my teeth.

NYARUBUYE (RWANDA)

bugs
flies
wagtails
lizards
bodies

wagtails peck at bugs
flies swarm
lizards skitter over bodies

bodies
dressed in sarongs
one in a blue dress
another in a pink dress with flowers
a tiny tot in flannel pyjamas
schoolboys in khaki shorts
a man in a green t-shirt with the name of an american restaurant chain
the slogan: *good friends closer than you think*

bodies
hundreds
scattered around the red-brick church
skulls picked clean
clothes sun-baked
bodies
some lie in the dirt some in the tall grasses one stares up into the out-
stretched arms of a marble Christ

the only sound
birds singing
the whine of swarming flies

inside the church
bodies
stacked in the aisles
crammed between the pews
bodies

twisted
arms thrown across their faces

on a step to the altar
a boy neatly boxed
      boxed in a cardboard food-aid container
the lid several feet away
      the label: *HARD BISCUIT*

a thousand dead a thousand a thousand a thousand
dead

the killers came in truckloads
they came from miles away
they bumped down a dirt track
they came from miles away

blasted shotguns tossed hand grenades hacked with gleaming blades

they left singing and shouting
we have smashed them at the church
smashed the wa-tutsi
smashed every last one

the boy in the box
look in the box
he's been hacked to pieces who
who will count the pieces

dig a pit for the dead
dig a pit and bury them
if the rock is volcanic dynamite it
bury them bury them from sight
      like so many rotting bulbs

but the church leaders decreed
(bury the dead and all is forgotten)
no one would line the bodies in rows
no one would transport them to pits
a thousand bodies would lie motionless
motionless as the maggots who are also
dead

the boy in the box
he could've been boxed up and mailed to oblivion
he will lie at the foot of the altar
a thousand bodies a shrine
a shrine to the void
they will not be dug into the earth
grass will not sprout from their ashes
they will lie there lie there

you can turn off your tv
        or keep it on
cameras will turn to sarajevo haifa the english channel diana
you can listen to pulp elastica oasis
you can sleep and wake up
nyarubuye will not disturb your dreams
the killers have fled live in camps
will revive their fortunes
(have already revived their fortunes)
kill kill and kill

what do the church leaders hope
(in el salvador a *campesino* was hacked to pieces
friends captured the soldiers made them
piece the *campesino* together made them
beg forgiveness from the murdered man)
the church leaders hope the killers will return
hope they will go to the boy in the box
go down on their knees beg forgiveness
beg forgiveness from every last one
this is what the church leaders

hope

IV

VI

STEPHEN'S HOUSE

Go to his house,

when you open his door, you will be greeted by a red pepper on the floor, no
longer looking like a bell, it is that shrivelled announcement before it rots
from the inside out,

the black leathery skins of banana peels lie along the wall like the delicate
script of Japanese calligraphy, no doubt offering the warmest of wel-
comes,

there is a book of his friend's selected poems, the new expanded edition,
leaning against the wall,

next to a Sainsbury's box of three pearl-white 100 watt light bulbs, there's
several brown paper bags with secondhand books bought with great
enthusiasm, but unopened,

there's unopened bills, several flyers offering bargains on pizza, a Tower
Hamlet's newspaper dated May 18, 1991,

at the end of the hall stands a wooden crate: it always gives me assurance
to see on it the empty *Café Creme* tin, which I left at his place twelve
years ago, in its undisturbed off-centre location.

Go to his house, step inside his kitchen,

you may find him waving around the nozzle of his vaccuum cleaner like a
Bedouin spirit dancer waving his prayer sticks, but do not be deceived,
he is sucking up the fruit flies,

he is taking cautious steps, the floor is covered with milk bottles and cartons
bloated with milk that has turned to greenish yoghurt,

egg cartons are stacked up along the cupboards and look like the Dalai
Lama's holy city of Lhasa,

there are bags full of bananas that have dried up like pieces of driftwood,
pocked with rust-coloured spots,

on the counter there is a jar which has balanced on its lid half an onion, the
various layers of skin are so dried out that they have separated, and
the onion looks like the lantern that Queequeg held at his boat's bow
beforethe Pequod, immersed in the foggiest darkness, plowed over it,

the rest of the counter is stacked with paper and plastic bags that have
been neatly flattened out before they joined the pile,

the top of the refrigerator is covered with a pile of charred matches which
resemble the ravages of open-pit mining,

he hasn't opened his refrigerator for six months,

if you go over to the sink, the sideboard is covered with rusty-brown broccoli
that looks like the forests of Max Ernst's frottages, grapefruit halves

that look like petrified flat mushrooms, the dried lopped-off ends of
parsnips, the bronzed discs of apple slices, celery which looks like his
favourite trees in St. James's Park (pick up the celery, smell its
pungent odours),

in the window, there's a plastic apple juice container with this most beautiful
scarlet flower bending from it, beside it an orange (go over and shake it,
even the seeds have turned to dust),

if you look out the window, which he is always wiping down with a wet cloth
to free it from the accumulated grime that muddies up most of London's
windows, you will see across the parking lot the mirror image of his
house, a balcony, a clothesline is strung up, saris and Sylheti silks flap
in the wind, the waft of curry and nutmeg floats out from the open door,
children dart in and around the drying laundry, beware! you might find
your London-cluttered mind drifting off to the banks of the Ganges,

he will carefully break your trance by offering you a tea, once he would pour
it from the angry spout of his kettle, but it now sits on the back
burner, broken, and he boils the water in his only pot, and because
there is not an inch of counter space, he will place the two cups,
precariously balanced, on one of the cooker rings,

he might let out a sigh, tell you that the local Thai restaurant has turned into
a Chicken McNugget, that he buys in food but he can never bring himself
to cook it, that last night he ate at an Indian restaurant where the great
Urdu poet Faiz Ahmed Faiz used to frequent when he visited London,

and then he might mutter a line that has recently been preoccupying him,
Pessoa's lovely line, 'There are ships moored in every poet'; from there
he will grow indignant with the warships currently anchored in the
Thames: what are they doing there? how different from the ships moored
in poets! or should a poet contain a few warships, too?

Go to his house, once he has handed you your tea — the only chair in the
kitchen is covered with the twisting paper of Digestive cookie packages
(he will mention, half-jokingly, that he intends to hang them as a
mobile: a paean to consumerist society), several bags of french bread
hard as truncheons, a book container with two slices of cucumber
dried on it like two owlish eyes —he will apologize that there is no
place to sit down, you will face each other, taking two sips, and then
he'll suggest going upstairs,

he will lead the way, you will notice that the door to his living room is open
less and less,

behind that door, furniture is stacked up like a funeral bargue: the furniture of
　　his mother who died last Christmas, who in his mind's eye he had
　　figured had another five years to live, who, as mother-swallow,
　　mother-song, mother-fish, mother-colour, mother-jasmine, mother-void,
　　will never again feed his emptiness with plum autumns, aniseed
　　horizons, ciabatta tenderness, polenta words, whose couch, perched
　　at the top, is turned upside down and its black belly, once the taut-
　　ness of drum skins, cries open with a gash,
once this room was dominated by an antique bookcase with glass doors, now
　　you can only walk around the path that makes its way between the
　　stack of furniture and the bookshelves that hug the walls,
walk the path, on the far side of the room, there is a pile of wood, collected
　　from the street, to feed the fire that used to warm wine-sodden binges
　　(friends would drop in and stay for three days, argue about Rimbaud's
　　syntax, the internal politics of the ANC, Thatcher's crushing of the
　　unions, the poll tax, recipes for homemade plonk, Goya's 'Los
　　Caprichos'), but the council installed central heating two years ago,
　　and, although Stephen has refused to turn on the central heating, he's
　　stopped using his fireplace,
walk the path that leads to the telephone, books and books and books, and
　　behind the first row of books, there is usually another: Albanian novels
　　nestle in with tracts on feminism, liberation theology, dance in Indian
　　culture, semiotics and, of course, poets — poets from Genoa, Mar-
　　seille, Vladivostok, Delhi, Kathmandu; poets from Beijing, Montevideo,
　　Valparaiso, Budapest, Kadango village; poets from Jakarta, Shanghai,
　　Itabara, Havanna, Reykjavik, Augsburg, Talitsy,
walk the other path, it is impossible to walk it, it leads to the windows, it is
　　stacked with rubbish bags from previous cleanups which he could not
　　bear to part with, light comes in through the parted blankets that
　　cover the windows, you can see traffic snaking up Commercial Road,
　　reaching maximum speed as it roars past his windows (double glazed
　　windows that once were open to let in the first scent of apple blos-
　　soms); you can see a spate of newly-constructed high-rise council
　　flats that have changed his view beyond recognition.

Go to his house, climb the stairs, on the right-hand side of every step, a
　　gathering of objects,
on the lowest step, a postcard leaning against the next step, a postcard of a
　　Greek village, two houses side by side, one is pink with white shutters,
　　the other is white with pink shutters, the photograph is black and

white except for the pink, a lone dog slinks past as if he was trying
not to disturb the tranquility of the houses,

on the next step, a card from one of the many libraries he frequents, a card
reminding him of four overdue books, he can renew them by telephone,
every night he promises himself that he'll renew them next day, but
two weeks have slipped by,

on the next step, a note on an index card printed in mauve crayon, WHERE
HAVE YOU BEEN? LOVE AMANDA (I can assure you that he will not
talk to you about the woman he loves, but who loves another; he will not
talk to you about the woman who loves him, but who he cannot love),

on the next step, a paper bag: inside, a pale blue-covered monograph on the
Russian poet Marina Tsvetayeva,

the next step, a book of the sixteenth century Spanish poet Gongora,

on the next, a peanut butter bottle full of peach pits,

the next, a stack of flyers advertizing a reading of Turkish poets at the
Approach Tavern,

the next, a black Twinings tea box with its sparse elaborations of gold hinting
at Oriental mystique (you will see these boxes nesting everywhere in
his innumerable bookshelves; they nest like birds on top of his books;
they are filled with index cards recording the bibliographical details of
every book of twentieth century poetry translated into English, and, if
that's not enough, he's undertaken to complete a bibliography of
every twentieth century novel translated into English),

in this box, his most recent compilations dug out from countless libraries
and secondhand bookshops and his own incomparable library of
poetry in translation which puts to shame the British Library's
collection: pull out some of the cards — never say this is the dry and
mechanical work of a plodding imagination — there is a whole world of
sustenance in the names: *The Horse Has Six Legs, Lyric Action and
Other Poems, A Splintered Mirror, Every Shut Eye Ain't Asleep, Capital of
Pain, The Error of Being, I Wear My Shadow Inside Me,* Grey Wolf Press,
Thunder's Mouth Press, Mudborn Press, Curbstone Press, Putu Oka
Sukanta, Miklos Radnoti, Ko Un, So Chong-Ju, Frantisek Halas,
Rabindranath Tagore, and so on,

on the top step, a toy carpenter's bench: six holes with six colourful pegs to
hammer into the holes, several times he has suggested that I take it
home to my twin sons, who, wild as mountain goats, greet him with a
hilarious 'Hello, fat chunk Stephen,' although he's as thin as the Bic
pen he writes with, he will chase after them, those two rascals who he
once referred to in one of his postcards to us as: 'How are the twin
Klebnikov's? How many revolutions have they recently spread?'

but the toy still rests at the top of the stairs, like the only bird in the sky, it is
        the only visible remembrance of his wife and five-year-old son who
        departed for India eight years ago, he could never stand in their way,
        his wife who was brought up in India, his wife who met him at Oxford
        beforehe spent three years as a shepherd on the windswept island of
        North Uist, his wife with her stones of common sense, he with a heart
        of bandaged sunlight and gannet sky.

Go to his house, stand on the landing,
crates once stuffed with Spanish onions or Seville oranges are stacked
        shoulder-height and stuffed with books,
to the right, his bathroom, wide as your outspread arms,
not a book in it, not a crate, not a tea box, not a paper bag, not a Digestive
        cookie package, not an apricot pit, not an egg carton, not a peanut
        butterjar, not the unspoken language of banana peels,
only a bathtub, and lined against the wall, a battalion of sponges and, at
        each end standing like sentries, Ajax containers,
and in the half-filled bathtub, jeans, underwear, socks and several mauve
        T-shirts which, having trapped air, look like bloated lunar lily pads,
last night he'd returned from a poetry reading at the Voice Box, the Bulgar-
        ian poet, Blaga Dimitrova, afterwards she had answered questions
        from the audience, so often the audience will clam up after some tin-
        head has posed an absurdly scholarly question about the title of
        some obscure poem which was not read that night, or any other night,
        but this time the dry crackly branch of pedantic scholarship was
        absent, the branch wore greenness, one man said he had no questions,
        but he just wanted to hear her continue to talk, and, in response to
        one of the questions, Blaga related how her home city had been
        bombed by the Allies at the end of the war, how she had been
        trapped in a basement, and years later when the Americans bombed
        Vietnam she felt compelled to express her sympathy, flew out to
        Vietnam for six months, returning to Sofia with an adopted daughter,
after the reading, Stephen, fired by the repore between the poet and the
        audience, was saddened, as always in these occasions, when everyone
        rushed home instead of plonking themselves on pub stools and
        continuing the evening,
he had walked through Soho, popped into a café on Bateman Street, just
        around the corner from where his mother had been born and his
        grandfather ran a café, he had a whiskey despite the fact that he was
        twenty years older than the mop-haired crowd who crammed into the
        café and jabbered about the Club Spangle, Wilkie Collins's Moonchild,

HUME CRONYN

silk blouses, art schools, contact sheets, Brixton, Nirvana, imagination, interactive visuals, paradise, God, American dentists, Radio 1,
arriving home, full of energy he dumped his clothes into the bathtub, but next morning his energy had deserted him, the fatigue of several years pulled down on his spine, he was simply incapable of wringing out the clothes and hanging them on the rope that extended the length of the bathroom.

Go to his house, the room on the right, it was once his son's bedroom,
take three steps inside: stacked-up furniture, bookshelves and boxes engulf the room, look at the chest of drawers missing their handles, the Indian vase which has a mouth of dust, the wardrobe with its mirror which is slowly being eaten away and looks like the cracked mudflats of the Mississippi River, bedframes, box springs, mattresses leaning against the wall,
ask him where the beds came from, he will tell you that a friend left one years ago, it was so long ago he can't remember who the friend was; and the other beds, he says, well, earth, wind and fire sleep on them, and the flood is around the corner,
somewhere, somewhere, somewhere his son's bed once occupied this room, where is it now? beneath the boxes? behind the mattresses? in the vase of dust? it sleeps inside his bones and squeezes his heart,
the cardboard boxes are stacked up, bedsheets and blankets tilt their crazy corners from the top, how many poems are coffined inside?
And the bookcases, of course, there are more bookcases (but the books here don't possess the careful tidiness of elsewhere: they seem more worn, the rag with which he dusts his books has not reached here, the spines of the books jut out in irregular formation, as if dreaming of the day he'll be possessed by one of their lines and pull them out to leaf through),
there's a predominance of French and German poets, you may be tempted to think that he orders his books by country, or language, but if you look closely, you will see interspersed between them an Italian novel, a Lebanese one, Canetti's sociological treatise on crowds, an anthology of Himalayan poetry, a post-structuralist work on Oedipus, folktales of Latin America, a pamphlet decrying the genocide of the Timorese people,
turn to your left, in the nook with bookshelves on either side defining the area, his desk,
on it, an old Olivetti typewriter: the tab for the letter r is missing — depending on his mood, he'll type a poem without the r, or if the spirit of

particularity is in him, each time an r is needed he will wrap his finger in a washcloth and press down the key (he jokes that one day he will compose a poem with a total absence of r's, or one using only an absence of r's);

on it, a piece of coloured glass worn down by the sea, a white stone that looks as if it is a piece of the Dead Sea scrolls, the sculpted leaf of a dandelion, a burr as large as a sea urchin, numerous letters he has not finished, a book review on the recently published biography of a Bengali poet, an article on Welsh poetry in translation, a stack of poems he is considering for inclusion in a human rights anthology he is editing, scraps of paper with possible titles for his own manuscript of poems,

like his refrigerator, he has not used his desk for six months,

even if he did clear off his desk, the encroaching furniture looms like a jaw that is about to snap,

he writes his poems sitting on the stairs, the stairs that climb up from the hallway that smells like rivers and fish, the stairs that aren't that steep but at moments appear like a chute he's about to plummet down, the 40 watt bulb a pitiful guarantee against the darkness.

Go to his house, the final room, his bedroom,

he will lead you through a maze of bookshelves, there's a small space beside his bed that seems like a veritable clearing, the floorboards seem to sparkle as if they've been freshly waxed, the grey blanket is adorned with the outspread wings of a Quetzalcoatl outlined in steeped white, surprisingly, a sweep of the hand smoothes out the crumpled look, two books lying face up on the blanket, oddly enough, seem to add to the impression of orderliness,

he will offer you a stool and will sit on the edge of the bed, and then he'll apologize, ask if you'd rather sit on the bed, he on the stool,

beside the bed, there's a large chest of drawers, on top of it a carefully placed row of books, I once counted twenty languages moving their lips in that single row of books,

in front of the chest of drawers, so that only the top drawer can open, a bookshelf: peeking midst a crowd of books stands a passport-sized photograph of his son, Michael, in a chequed shirt and tie (for the past three years Michael and his mother, returned from India, have lived outside of Oxford — Stephen will visit them when he can, and if in one of those unrestrained moods of intimacy you ask him, how does he feel about missing Michael's childhood? he will say that he doesn't think about it, but you feel that behind that statement there is a darkness that, if he began to fall, there would be nothing to break the fall, so he makes every attempt not to begin to fall),

behind you there are crates of books stacked to shoulder height, behind that large packing boxes, and behind that more bookshelves that rise up to the curtained windows, 'Is it too dark for you?' he'll ask, but it's a real effort for him to stand between the crates, go onto tiptoes, reach over the boxes, bookshelves, grab hold of the curtain and rip it partially open,

on the floor, there's a white container that looks like a cookie tin, Delft-blue letters spell out *flour,* there is a windmill below the letters, and when ever he starts one of his many cleanups, he takes a cloth and, lifting off the lid, dusts it as if he was polishing a diamond (inside are folded pieces of paper, envelopes, brown paper bags, pieces of cereal boxes, all covered with crabbed writing),

this is his piggy bank, this is his deposit box, this is his wealth: this is where he deposits his poems (how many has he lost: stuffed in boxes, on envelopes, between the pages of books, on tissue?)

'It's a crime!!!' one of his friends, who doesn't for one moment believe in the exalted place of poetry, had screamed at him, 'you can't throw out a single match head, but you literally throw away your poems,' and he had suggested that Stephen find a container where he could deposit his poems as soon as he entered the door or finished one of his sojourns on the stairs,

but of course there's numerous drafts, they will not all fit into his flour tin, the last draft of the poem to his mother, the poem written on the platform of Westminister station, the poem written in Lord Rodney's Head, oh where, oh where, oh where are they? a few were in a school locker where he taught two years ago, but of course the school cleaned out his locker.

Poems, poems and poems, go to his house,

there's a poem by the Indonesian poet, Charil Anwar, that begins, 'My house is built of heaped-up poems...' — write it on a piece of paper and tack it on his front door,

Stephen has a friend who, when he gets drunk, will stand on one leg like a stork and shout at him, shout that Stephen will never be a poet until he gives up his house and lives in the street,

Stephen's eyes will light up with a glimmer, there is only humour in his reply, not the glinting shininess of cleverness, 'I've brought the street into my house,'

every six months the council notifies him that they will be spraying to stem the cockroach infestation,

for weeks he'll lose sleep, you might find him standing in the kitchen sucking
up the fruit flies — Oh, Don Quixote with your lance, the vacuum cleaner
— things will be pushed this way and that, the flour tin will be dusted, a
few more rubbish bags will make their way to the living room like
pear-shaped men who have grown too fat to budge,

the pest-contol men will come, amazingly no mention is made of the
overgrowth, they will spray, if the space along the baseboards isn't
clear, they will just shoot the spray into the air,

dioxin, dioxin, dioxin, you inhabit the cushions, the mattresses, the stacks of
paper, cardboard boxes, you inhabit and inhabit and inhabit, emitting
poisons in slow gasps,

how often he is ill with flu, fatigue weighs down his soul as if he was carrying
an elephant on his back, six months he has been waiting for his hernia
operation,

but still there's a reading of Portuguese language poets in Manchester he will
make the trip for, even though they are reading in London in a week's
time, he cannot bear to see them in the soulless Voice Box, he will drag
himself to the last showing of Mandala, a Korean film, that he has
already seen twice, he will drag himself to a reading of Somali poets in
Bethnal Green, he will drag himself to his solitudinous mornings in the
Lord Rodney's Head in Whitechapel to write his journal, to a Bengali
family's house in Shadwell to edit a book of poems by their 14-year-old
son who died last year of leukemia, he will drag himself to a memorial
service at SOAS for the Chinese poet Gu Cheng,

talk to him about Gu Cheng, Gu Cheng who wore the cut-off legs of trousers
as hats to ward off an alien language threatening to invade his skull,
who murdered his wife with a tomahawk on the southern-most island
of New Zealand the day her lover was arriving from Germany, and then
hung himself from a tree outside of their house (a poet can sacrifice
himself to the word, at any moment of the day the music can grow in
him, but ask him to drive to the station, peel a potato, burp the baby,
fill out tax forms, fetch Bach flower remedies from the nearest herbal
shop, and he can't do it, he can't drive a car, wield a potato peeler,
burp the baby, tax forms are incomprehensible, who has time for the
body? the nerve ends have reached out of the body like a flow of
electrons reaches out from a tree to welcome the lightning).

Go to his house, an ordinary night (what is an ordinary night?), he will most
likely be listening to the world service at three, tonight they are reading
Wole Soyinka's letter from Nigeria,

the picture of Michael falls to the floor,

his book of poems is dedicated to his wife,

his daughter, what was her name? I have known Stephen longer than my tin of
   Café Creme has sat on his onion crate, and still he has never mentioned
   her name,

we keep things to ourselves, we bring more and more of the world into us, it's
   too difficult to clean out the past, behind the couch, between the
   pages, inside the broken kettle, what will we find? (shake the orange!
   even the seeds have turned to dust),

but this is a seed which has not turned to dust: that night, in the first years of
   their marriage, he had run from their house, the shadows were the milky
   white of apple blossoms, his wife had called the ambulance, the
   ambulance had not come, had not come, had not come, the hospital
   had assured them that it was on the way, the hospital was only three
   minutes ride by taxi, he ran out onto the street, his ten-day-old
   daughter pulled to his chest, the blossoms, the blossoms, the
   blossoms, their first day, and she died in his arms, in his arms, in the
   taxi, 'Don't take her away from me, from us, from us,' he cried,

he once described that taxi ride as the longest journey in her brief life: some
   people travel to Bombay, Timbuktu, Rio de Janeiro, Anchorage, some
   several times around the world, her heart gave out before she finished
   her three minute journey,

do not say that a house is the mind, or the mind is a house, who can talk
   about a life, look from one angle it appears tragic, overgrown, too
   weighty, not weighty enough, lost, confused, abused, abusing, look
   from another angle, it is gifted, it celebrates, it jokes, it loves, what
   more can I tell you about his house: one more thing! some mornings
   there is only one light on, it burns as pale as a moon in a 10 am sky,
   other mornings there is a flotilla of suns, and that house, that house,
   that house is ablaze.